Published 2021 by Like A Stack Of Books

About Mr. Yary
Yary Livan

Yary Livan is a living Cambodian Ceramics master who works in Lowell, Massachusetts where he lives with his family. Yary studied at the University of Fine Arts in Phnom Penh, where he learned ceramics from the old masters. Yary has a ceramics studio in Lowell and spends time teaching both children and adults in his community and at a local community college. In his community he is known affectionately as "Mr. Yary" by all. In 2012 Yary also partnered with longtime friend and fellow master ceramist Kang Proeung to build a wood-fired kiln, using space provided by Lowell National Historic Park in a partnership with Middlesex Community College. He was honored in 2015 by the National Endowment for the Arts as a National Heritage Fellow.

About the Author

Jennifer Stack is a PreK teacher in the Lowell Public Schools in Lowell, MA. After a fruitless search for Cambodian Children's books, she decided to write her own. Jennifer lives in Massachusetts with her husband Mike, daughter Catherine, and tuxedo cat Bronx. When she's not teaching, she is an avid knitter, baker, and handbell ringer. She has always loved children's books and it has always been her dream to write one!

This book is dedicated to Mr. Yary and the Summer 2021 Cambodian Ceramics and Culture class of the Lowell Teacher Academy as well as my Cambodian families. You are inspiring!

Mr. Yary Makes Cambodian Ceramics

Written by Jennifer Stack
Illustrated by Angel Toba

Can you turn a lump of clay into a beautiful elephant pot? My friend Mr. Yary can. He learned to make beautiful pieces from the old Cambodian Masters a long time ago, and now he teaches other people how to work with clay too.

Mr. Yary lives and works in Lowell, Massachusetts. He has a pottery studio where he makes all of his artwork. Mr. Yary is also a teacher. He loves to teach kids and adults how to work with clay. All the kids and adults love Mr. Yary.

350mm

5mm

6

To make clay, you need to work with lots of different kinds of tools. Mr. Yary is creative and makes some of his own tools. For a scraper, he takes a saw blade from the hardware store and sands it down to make a fine point. He also likes to use pencils for carving. There's no better tool than your own fingers though! You can't lose those!

There are rules Mr. Yary teaches so that your pots will turn out properly. The clay has to be wet and soft to shape and carve, so you can add water if the clay is too dry. If you don't keep the clay soft, your pot will crack and be hard to carve. Sometimes Mr. Yary starts his work with a slab of clay, which is a flat piece he makes using a special roller.

Sometimes Mr. Yary starts his work on a pottery wheel, which spins as he works to help him make smooth and round shapes.

When you work on a table from a slab, you can use a heavy piece of cloth to keep the clay from sticking to your table. There is a special kind of glue, called slip, that you need to use to stick pieces together. Slip is made from dried clay mixed with water and it has a muddy texture. You have to score, or cut into the parts to give the slip something to hold onto and make your join strong. Then you can use a wet sponge to smooth out the joins.

Mr. Yary adds traditional Khmer decorations to his pots. There are flowers, plants, leaves, and geometric patterns. Using the old patterns is a way that Mr. Yary keeps his cultural traditions alive and how he shares them with the world.

After the pots are dried,
Mr. Yary adds glazes.
These are special paints
that turn different colors
when they go into a very
hot oven, called a kiln.
He uses different colors to
make the patterns show
up better on the pots.

Next, the magic of the kiln firing can happen. Mr. Yary and his friend built a special wood fire kiln near his studio in Lowell using bricks. It was built in 2012 on land that is part of the Lowell National Historic Park. He built it just like the kilns that were used in Cambodia many years ago. It takes many hours to fire the pottery pieces, and so Mr. Yary's special kiln even has a spot where you can cook some dinner or a pizza!

There are special cones inside of the kiln that burn down so that Mr. Yary knows how hot it is. He can add more wood or stop adding wood to control the temperature inside.

This is important because if the kiln does not get hot enough, the glaze will be dry and rough and the piece will not get stronger. If the kiln gets too hot the clay can change shapes or even melt!

This could break the kiln, so Mr. Yary has to be really careful to protect his beautiful pieces and the pottery by controlling the fire.

When the pieces are done firing, they have to cool, and then Mr. Yary takes them back to his studio. Some lucky customers are able to buy them and bring them home to enjoy.

Sometimes Mr. Yary makes special pieces for his beautiful garden.
One day I visited his garden and he had brought home a little blue turtle and a big golden pot to place near the pond in his garden! Maybe someday you will be lucky enough to come take a class with Mr. Yary and learn all about Cambodian Ceramics.

Lightning Source UK Ltd.
Milton Keynes UK
UKHW051847110821
388659UK00002B/23